# FINDING MY CALM

Hardie Grant acknowledges the Traditional Owners of the Country on which we work, the Wurundjeri People of the Kulin Nation and the Gadigal People of the Eora Nation, and recognises their continuing connection to the land, waters and culture. We pay our respects to their Elders past and present.

Wildling Books
Hardie Grant Children's Publishing
Wurundjeri Country
Level 11, 36 Wellington Street
Collingwood Victoria 3066
Melbourne | Sydney | San Francisco
hardiegrant.com/childrens

ISBN: 9781761214738
First published in Australia in 2025

Printed and bound in HeShan China, November 2025
by LEO Paper Products LTD.

The paper this book is printed on is from FSC® certified forests and other controlled sources. FSC® promotes environmentally responsible, socially beneficial and economically viable management of the world's forests.

4 6 7 5 3

# FINDING MY CALM

REBEKAH LIPP · CRAIG PHILLIPS

I like being me
a small person, like **YOU**

There's lots to be learned
and some **GROWING** to do.

But being small can be tricky
when you're put in a PICKLE

So I've a RHYME that'll help,
a quick fix for those niggles.

'Wake up, out of bed
rise and shine, SLEEPYHEAD!

Up you get and get **DRESSED**
you've a **BIG** day ahead.'

But, I hadn't slept right
I woke up in a GRUMP

And SLUMPED from my bunk
met the day with a HUMPH!

Well, my socks were a cinch
the trousers – no trouble

But my jacket had … buttons!
Oh no! What a BOGGLE.

My fingers were **FUDDLED**
they'd somehow forgot

How to do up my buttons
I'd **MESSED** up the lot.

The more they criss-crossed the **CROSSER** I got

With that **MUDDLE** of buttons and my front all in knots.

But then I count loud,

'FIVE, FOUR, THREE, TWO, ONE!'

And remember a rhyme
for FINDING MY CALM.

'*What is it?*' you wonder.
Well, I'm here to tell
Tell you all about that **RHYME**
then you'll know it as well!

Five things I can **SEE**! Four things I can **FEEL**!
Three things I can **HEAR**! Two things I can **SMELL**!

I'm almost there
I'm feeling **GREAT**!

Now, last of all
one thing I can **TASTE**!

See how I've **GROWN**
and how far I've come.

With help from that handy
**'FIVE, FOUR, THREE, TWO, ONE!'**

With practice, you'll see …
it works like a CHARM
It's just the right rhyme
for FINDING YOUR CALM!

'It's a BIG day, I know
and you've come oh so far

Even did up your **BUTTONS**
nearly there … Here we are!'

But as we pulled up
my school – it seemed BIGGER

And the BUSTLE of kids
sent my heart all a-wither.

I bargained … **IMPLORED**
gave my all just to stall

But the rush swept me up
through the door, down the hall.

I'm just LITTLE, you know
a small person, that's all

As that bustle got bigger
I felt smaller than small.

The more kids that filed in
the more **FLUMMOXED** I got
With the hustle and **HURRY**
of the first-day school-drop.

But then I count loud,

'FIVE, FOUR, THREE, TWO, ONE!'

And remember a rhyme
for FINDING MY CALM.

Now let's you and me
rhyme it right from the start

'Til we've got it down pat
and we know it by **HEART**.

Five things I can **SEE**! Four things I can **FEEL**!
Three things I can **HEAR**! Two things I can **SMELL**!

I'm almost there
I'm feeling **GREAT!**

Now, last of all
one thing I can **TASTE!**

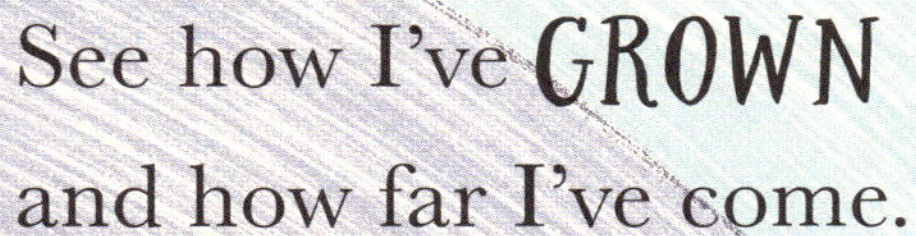

See how I've GROWN
and how far I've come.

With help from that handy
'FIVE, FOUR, THREE, TWO, ONE!'

With practice, you'll see …
it works like a charm

It's just the right rhyme
for FINDING YOUR CALM!

'There'll be GAMES today
with pretending and PLAY

So pitch in and play **FAIR**
and play the right way.'

I'd done all my buttons
the school drop-off, too

Now, who likes games?
Well – I do! That's **WHO**!

But games need rules
or they'll wind up a **MESS**

When it comes to pretend
I bet I know **BEST**!

I'm CHIEF of all games
couldn't they see?

The best way to PLAY
is to listen to me.

And did they? you ask
oh NO – they did NOT

And the less they listened
the HOTTER I got!

But then I count loud,
'FIVE, FOUR, THREE, TWO, ONE!'

And remember a rhyme
for FINDING MY CALM.

Let's try it again
fix that **RHYME** in our minds
So we'll remember it well
call it up any time.

Five things I can SEE! Four things I can FEEL!
Three things I can HEAR! Two things I can SMELL!

I'm almost there
I'm feeling **GREAT**!

Now, last of all
one thing I can **TASTE**!

See how I've **GROWN**
and how far I've come.

With help from that handy
**'FIVE, FOUR, THREE, TWO, ONE!'**

I feel **PROUD** as punch
and taller than tall!

'Cause I'll rhyme any time
I feel **TROUBLED** at all.

With practice, you'll see …
it works like a CHARM
It's just the right rhyme
for FINDING YOUR CALM!

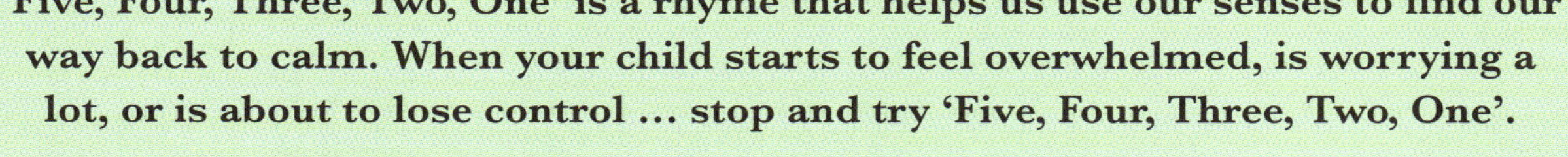

# PARENT/TEACHER NOTES

**'Five, Four, Three, Two, One' is a rhyme that helps us use our senses to find our way back to calm. When your child starts to feel overwhelmed, is worrying a lot, or is about to lose control ... stop and try 'Five, Four, Three, Two, One'.**

## FIVE THINGS YOU CAN SEE

Take a deep breath and, using your eyes, LOOK. Describe five things that you can see. Take your time and use facts to carefully describe each one. For example, I see a big dog with long brown hair and brown eyes, and its tongue is sticking out. Use the book and find five things you can see. Try to find different things each time you read the book. Then take a moment to look around where you are and try to describe five things you can see.

## FOUR THINGS YOU CAN FEEL

Take a deep breath and, using your body, FEEL. Describe four things you can feel. It could be the chair you are sitting on or the clothing you are wearing. You could even pick up something that might feel interesting to touch and describe how it feels. For example, I can feel the book that I am holding. It feels smooth. Try to imagine what things you could feel as you read the story.

## THREE THINGS YOU CAN HEAR

Take a deep breath and, using your ears, LISTEN. Describe three things you can hear. Be still and quiet and really tune in to your surroundings. What do you hear? It could be birds chirping or the wind rustling in the trees. Look through the pages of this book and imagine what you might hear. It could be the dog barking or children laughing.

## TWO THINGS YOU CAN SMELL

Take a deep breath and, using your nose, SMELL. Describe two things you can smell. We usually don't take time to smell things unless the smell is really strong. Really take your time and see if you can smell anything new. It could be the smell of the play dough you were playing with or the smell of the grass that has just been mowed. Have a look through the book and try to imagine what smells you might notice as you read the story.

## ONE THING YOU CAN TASTE

Take a deep breath and, using your mouth, TASTE. Describe one thing you can taste. You might need to actually get something to eat, or you might still be able to taste the last thing you ate. Slowly eat something and really notice how it tastes. Try not to think of anything else, just notice the taste of what you are eating. Look through the book and imagine the things you might be able to eat as you read.

# WHAT IS MINDFULNESS?

Mindfulness helps to bring our attention into the present moment, so we are not thinking about the past, worrying about the future or swept up in emotions or thoughts in the now. Our mind is fully focused on one thing. Often our thoughts can distract our mind and cause us to not be present in what we are doing. How often do you eat dinner and really focus on how the food tastes by bringing your full attention to your meal? We live in a world that is in a constant state of rushing, and mindfulness is about slowing down and enjoying the moments we have right now.

Teaching mindfulness to our children, so they can use it on a daily basis, can lead to a host of benefits for them including reduced stress levels and alleviating anxiety and depression. It helps children learn to respond to their feelings in a healthy way and makes them less likely to lash out, providing peace, calm and increased levels of happiness and joy.

## WAYS TO PRACTISE MINDFULNESS

### BREATHING

Sit still and take a deep breath in through your nose until your belly fills up, then pause and hold, and then, pretending you are blowing out of a straw through your mouth, slowly exhale. Try this four or fives times and see if you feel more relaxed.

### BODY SQUEEZE

Standing up tall, tighten all the muscles you can in your body, even your face. Squeeze them for as long as you can. Then slowly relax your muscles. You can try doing different parts of your body and slowly working your way down from your head to your feet.

## BLOW SOME BUBBLES

Bubbles are fun and hard not to be mesmerised by. Blowing out the bubbles can help relax you with some mindful breathing. See how many you can blow and then chase and pop them, or just watch them drift away, seeing how high they get.

## MINDFUL NATURE WALK

Take a short walk and really notice and take in your surroundings. Try the 'Five, Four, Three, Two, One' whilst out for a walk.

# MORE WILDLING BOOKS!

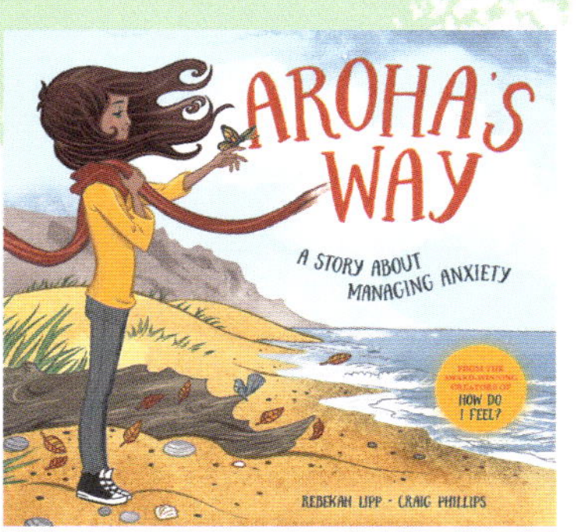


## AROHA'S WAY

Come along on a journey with Aroha as she wards off nervousness, fear, worrying thoughts and apprehension. Full of simple yet effective tools that everyone can use including exercise, belly breathing, mindfulness, connecting with others and sharing our worries.

## AROHA KNOWS

Spending time in nature makes Aroha feel all kinds of wonderful emotions. Aroha and her friends experience the joy of nature and explore how it can benefit our wellbeing.

## AROHA'S CHOICE

Our brains help us think, learn, and do all sorts of amazing things! Aroha learns that she can use her thoughts to influence her emotions in a positive way and help overcome negative feelings.

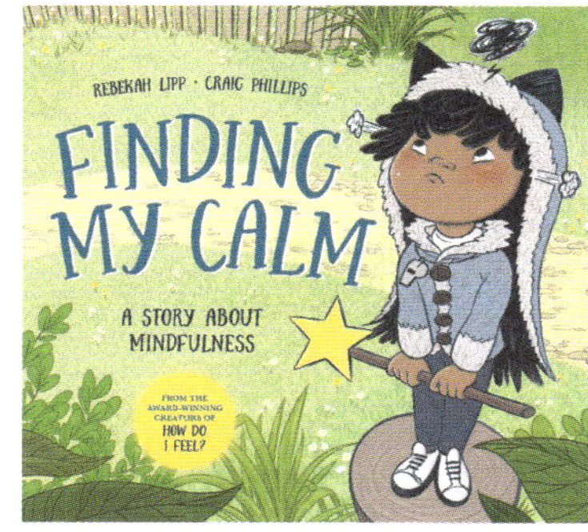


## FINDING MY CALM

Learn mindfulness and build the confidence to overcome stressful moments through fun, memorable rhyme!

## LET IT GO

Join Aroha and her friends as they navigate their way through four emotions (sadness, anger, shame and fear) by finding unique ways to release their feelings.

## BIG EMOTIONS FOR LITTLE PEOPLE

The perfect introduction to emotions big and small!

# ABOUT WILDLING BOOKS

**Wildling Books inspire, delight and empower children. Every storybook and resource can be used as a conversation-starter to explore emotional literacy, promote well-being, and help navigate every young wildling's unique inner world.**

## HOW DO I FEEL? A DICTIONARY OF EMOTIONS FOR CHILDREN

An essential emotional literacy tool for children with 60+ definitions inside!

## LET IT FLOW

Learn how to channel your emotional energy in healthy, safe ways in this accessible guide for children.

## ABOUT THE AUTHOR

**Rebekah Lipp** is an author, entrepreneur and mental health advocate residing in New Zealand. She co-wrote *Finding Gratitude* (Quarto, 2019). Her personal journey with anxiety and depression and knowledge of cognitive behavioural therapy (CBT) inspired Wildling Books, alongside her passion to bring awareness to children's mental health, emotional well-being and anxiety. With a gentle parenting approach, Rebekah feels that all children have genius within them and if we act out of a place of compassion, kindness and love, we will see our children thrive.

## ABOUT THE ILLUSTRATOR

**Craig Phillips** is an award-winning illustrator whose art has appeared in published works, anthologies and exhibitions across the world. He worked on Neil Gaiman's *American Gods* and his first solo work, *Giants, Trolls, Witches, Beasts* won the New Zealand Book Award's Russell Clark Award for Illustration, an Australian Gold Ledger, a CBCA Notable and was a finalist in the Aurealis Awards. Craig lives and works in New Zealand.